AF552930

Leap of Faith

Leap of Faith

Sumer Sethi, MD

Published by
PRABHAT PRAKASHAN PVT. LTD.
4/19 Asaf Ali Road,
New Delhi-110 002 (INDIA)
e-mail: prabhatbooks@gmail.com

ISBN 978-93-5322-844-6
LEAP OF FAITH
by Shri Sumer Sethi, MD

Edition —
2025

Price
₹ 200.00 (Rupees Two Hundred only)

Printed at
R-Tech Offset Printers, Delhi

FOREWORD

I am delighted to write this foreword, not only because Dr. Sumer Sethi is my husband as well my colleague but also because I believe deeply that Dr. Sumer Sethi is unlike most motivational writers in two ways. First, he treats training the mind and body as a technological challenge rather than moral imperative. Second, he somehow manages to be an inspirational role model and believes in "If you can't, you must. If you must, you can."

Motivational books are usually about taking immediate action. By contrast, this book is a bit more, well, thoughtful. It explains how your thoughts mould your personality, and how that personality drives you to take action and determines the type of action you'll take.

A big part of motivation is clearing your mind of the clutter that weighs it down. Dr. Sumer Sethi helps you differentiate between what's really important and deserving of your attention and what's just 'noise in the system'. According to him Stress is nothing more than a socially acceptable form of mental illness.

In this pioneering book Dr. Sethi shares what he has learned and provides a comprehensive framework on positive thinking filled with proven principles, compelling stories, practical ideas and practices that will help anyone become an optimistic.

In Captivate, he shares shortcuts, systems, and secrets for taking charge of your mind in any situation.

I feel honoured and privileged to have this opportunity to write the foreword of Dr. Sumer Sethi's book. Looking at this magnificent volume I am absolutely amazed at Dr. Sethi's this work which is a mine of information and a great source of inspiration for everyone. In short I would like to say that Dr. Sethi's this book is unique and surely a work to treasure. So read it, enjoy it and learn from it. Thank you Dr. Sumer for writing such a masterpiece.

—Dr. Deepti Sethi

PREFACE

Idea behind this book began with an invitation to speak on a Tedx talk in Bhopal. I started to think about what has made all the difference for me in my journey so far. In that zone of introspection, I began jotting down notes in my phone notebook for the talk and compilation of those notes is in your hands today as a book.

I discovered the role our subconscious judgement plays in the decisions we make. Life offers us choices and how we go about them makes all the difference. In the first chapter of this book, I have talked about the nudges, a concept which is very close to my heart. I believe we are all guided by our subconscious nudges or so called gut feeling. In this section I have tried to introspect my own life decisions and those of some famous people. I believe we all resonate best at a particular frequency at which we would make the maximum impact and if we are off track we feel the gentle nudge towards the path. Even picking up this book today by you I believe is a subconscious nudge and you tend to pick up books when you need them most and let me express my gratitude that you decided to give me an opportunity to share with you my ideas and I believe reading a book is like having a conversation with author and I can already imagine sitting and chatting with you over a coffee and discussing.

Life, however, is not a predetermined course and you always have the freedom to select your course. Decision to follow the subconscious nudge based on the blurred picture it offers is what I have called as the leap of faith. Many people feel the nudges towards their destined frequencies but not all take the leap of faith. That is why I have used this as the title of this book as well. Courage and ability to take the leap when it matters the most, makes all the difference.

What next, not all who take the leap make a huge impact, many of them give up because of fear and pain in the path. That is where the third chapter comes in about passion. The mad driving force towards the goal, ability to relentlessly work towards your cause with enthusiasm. That energy is third ingredient which propels you forward.

In the long run passion may wear out and once you are on your own, when nothing else seems to drive you, the final ingredient holds you and takes you forward and that is purpose. That is the final chapter in the book.

I have kept the book short and to the point and I hope to regain the love I got from the readers of my last book 'Fire in the Belly'.

Whatever I have learnt is through my journey of mentoring lacs of medical students and doctors in their careers as a part of Delhi Academy of Medical Sciences and I am forever grateful to all my students of past, present and future.

I present you this book with a prayer, that you get the power to feel the nudges when the subconscious pushes you to your destined path of maximum impact, I hope you get the courage to take the leap of faith when it matters the most, I wish you can then propel your Journey forward with passion and hopefully find purpose in your journey.

Amen

I look forward to continuing this conversation even after you have finished reading this book through my social media handle and would love to hear your story as well.

ACKNOWLEDGEMENTS

My Parents Dr. Subhash Chander Sethi and Mrs. Karuna Sethi for being a constant source of encouragement and inspiration throughout.

My wife Dr. Deepti Sethi for her support and patience without which this project would never have been possible. My son Krish for bearing with me in the manuscript preparation. Your support is my backbone.

Thanking you for blessings and support Mr. Deepak Bahl and Mrs. Geeta Bahl.

Dr. Sidharth Kumar Sethi, Dr. Shilpa Singla, Ms. Sumati, Mr. Sameer Bahl and Ms. Adity Bahl for the wishes and support. Dr. Rajiv Bhagi for all his support always.

Mr. Aayush Sharma for his immense contribution in getting everything organised meticulously and always believing in the possibility of this book.

Contents

	Foreword	*5*
	Preface	*9*
	Acknowledgements	*13*
1.	Nudges	19
2.	Leap of Faith	37
3.	Passion	49
4.	Purpose	77

Leap of Faith

NUDGES

My thoughts regarding this post began one day when I was driving and tuning my radio to a popular FM station 93.5. While tuning I could hear the music play at frequencies around the channel but it was noisy and only when I tuned into the channel the music was clear and was just the way it was supposed to be. Then, I wondered about life, how many of us are trapped into frequencies which apparently are playing the music but the real joy is missing because of the noise.

What if some of us have no idea on how the correct channel would sound like, would continue listening to noisy channels for life and keep wondering why the pleasure is missing even though you can hear the music.

There lies the secret to the world. If the music is not perfect, if there is too much noise, even if you are not aware of how the perfect feels like, you will feel gentle nudges, pushing you to the right channel.

These nudges begin by the feeling of uneasiness, that feeling that tells you something isn't right. Something needs to be done.

Some people become accustomed to wrong channel. They become ok with the status quo. They ask what if we lose this music with change. At least we have something. They ignore the nudges. They know something is not right. But they stick to their journey. They start building subconscious regret.

All people who are in high achievement zone would acknowledge that sometimes in their life they experienced the nudges. They were alert enough to respond.

Each Nudge pushed them towards the frequency where they would resonant in sync with their destined frequencies.

That's is where magic begins.

"There is a tide in the affairs of men, which taken at the flood, leads on to fortune. Omitted, all the voyage of their life is bound in shallows and in miseries. On such a full sea are we now afloat. And we must take the current when it serves, or lose our ventures."

—William Shakespeare"

This led me to explore more and try to understand the value of nudges in a high achiever's life. Do they all know their destination from the start. Story books written after the journey is over seem to suggest so.

I began by introspecting. Did I know where would I reach when I was in my school. Do I still know, where I am headed? First nudge I had was joining radiology after graduation. In the initial allotment after graduation I selected neurosurgery in AIIMS Delhi, top place and top branch. People congratulated me and if everyone thinks it is right, it must be right, was my thought process. But two months into the branch I started to get that feeling of uneasiness. Destiny started to nudge me away from it. I was a more cerebral, analytical person and found myself enjoying images more than The surgery part and ended up resigning and joining radiology. Last year when I was nominated in top 14 global radiology educators in world. I wondered what if I had ignored the nudges at that stage. It is not that I would not have done well as neurosurgeon, but somehow, that exact matchup between the person I was and what I was doing was not happening. I often attribute whatever I have done in life to my ability feel the nudges and respond to them.

Similar nudge I felt when I started enjoying teaching and DAMS (leading medical education institute in India, 250plus branches) happened. One of my seniors from college met me on the road next to Karol Bagh metro station (where DAMS head office is today) and asked me why was I wasting my time and career by pursuing this. It didn't make sense to him and probably to anyone at that time. Now, with 250 plus centres across the country and India's fastest growing medical education app launch I wonder what if I had heard what people were saying instead of listening to nudges what would you have done, would you even be reading this book.

Then, do you feel the nudges in relationships as well. One fine day I was sitting on night call in college cafe, I don't remember thinking about what, she walked in and I felt a nudge to talk. It could have ended anyhow but we ended up talking all night. Years later after we got married I asked my wife about this day and to my surprise she went home and told her mom about this, and she felt we would eventually get married. She felt the nudge too. What people call as love at first sight, is probably our subconscious recognizing something important, which our conscious understanding is yet to perceive or acknowledge. That nudges us.

Is it that destiny helps us by suggesting what path is best suited to us. But then leaves us with choice of either following the nudges or remain on a rigid path. That choice to me is the one which determines our '*karma*', yes you are free to make your choices, select your own path but be open enough, be receptive enough to feel the gentle nudges of the destiny trying to help you be on the path of your destiny, the path where you make the maximum impact.

Subconscious plays a big role in this. We have two thinking processes, conscious and subconscious. Conscious is the one which is concerned with detailed and precise thinking, while subconscious is faster, but creates a quick blurred picture without details. Imagine when someone asks you about a shop in a street, you have never visited that shop but passed by that street, but never consciously gave it thought. But when someone asks about it you are able to conjure a quick image and answer that is your subconscious speaking. Sometimes you say that everything is alright it is the way you want it to be but your subconscious doesn't agree and creates a conflict. That creates the uneasiness and nudges you to change. Change to a different frequency. Often you will hear it in the movies as my brain and heart are

saying two different things. Or you will hear people talk about gut feeling.

"We Must Be Willing To Get Rid of the Life We've Planned, So As To Have the Life That Is Waiting for Us."

—Joseph Campbell"

Those of us looking for new options for ourselves are challenged to let go of some of the life planned by our status quo—that often creates the mismatch between the heart and the mind.

However, subconscious is not always a good thing. Sometimes it leads us to prejudices and often we get biased by stereotypes. Gradually by practise to hear your inner voice, your subconscious you have to eliminate thoughts due to previous prejudice. These prejudices may lead to missing out on something useful on one side and may lead to extreme practises like racism on the other end of the spectrum.

Then I wonder if these nudges played a role in high achievers that we know of. I decided to do a bit of research, by looking into life of some of the most famous scientists and entrepreneurs that we know of. Did they know from the start what would be their destination, did they start keeping the end in mind, or, were they nudged in the way. Nudges towards a destiny that would make them immortal.

Let me start by discussing few landmark men of science. There is a term in science called as 'Serendipity'.

Alexander Fleming

By 1927, Fleming had been investigating the properties of staphylococci. He was already well known from his earlier work, and had developed a reputation as a brilliant researcher, but his laboratory was often untidy. On 3 September 1928, Fleming returned to his laboratory having spent

August on holiday with his family. Before leaving, he had stacked all his cultures of staphylococci on a bench in a corner of his laboratory. On returning, Fleming noticed that one culture was contaminated with a fungus, and that the colonies of staphylococci immediately surrounding the fungus had been destroyed, whereas other staphylococci colonies farther away were normal, famously remarking 'That's funny'. Fleming grew the mould in a pure culture and found that it produced a substance that killed a number of disease-causing bacteria. He identified the mould as being from the genus Penicillium, and, after some months of calling it 'mould juice', named the substance it released penicillin. Fleming's discovery of penicillin changed the world of modern medicine by introducing the age of useful antibiotics; penicillin has saved, and is still saving, millions of people around the world.

He felt the nudge to explore something unusual and was doing something else, and ended up making history.

In his own words, "One sometimes finds, what one is not looking for. When I woke up just after dawn on September 28, 1928, I certainly didn't plan to revolutionize all medicine by discovering the world's first antibiotic, or bacteria killer. But I suppose that was exactly what I did."

Wilhelm Röntgen

During 1895, Röntgen was investigating the external effects from the various types of vacuum tube equipment when an electrical discharge is passed through them. In early November, he was repeating an experiment with one of vacuum tubes in which a thin aluminium window had been added to permit the cathode rays to exit the tube but a cardboard covering was added to protect the aluminium from damage by the strong electrostatic field that produces the cathode rays. He knew the cardboard covering prevented light from escaping, yet Röntgen observed that the invisible cathode rays caused a fluorescent effect on a small cardboard screen painted with barium platinocyanide when it was placed close to the aluminium window.

In the late afternoon of 8 November 1895, Röntgen was determined to test his idea. He carefully constructed a black cardboard covering similar to the one he had used on the earlier tube. He covered the Crookes–Hittorf tube with the cardboard and attached electrodes to a Ruhmkorff coil to generate an electrostatic charge. Before setting up the barium platinocyanide screen to test his idea, Röntgen darkened the room to test the opacity of his cardboard cover. As he passed the Ruhmkorff coil charge

through the tube, he determined that the cover was light-tight and turned to prepare the next step of the experiment. It was at this point that Röntgen noticed a faint shimmering from a bench a few feet away from the tube. To be sure, he tried several more discharges and saw the same shimmering each time.

Röntgen speculated that a new kind of ray might be responsible. 8 November was a Friday, so he took advantage of the weekend to repeat his experiments and made his first notes. In the following weeks he ate and slept in his laboratory as he investigated many properties of the new rays he temporarily termed 'X-rays', using the mathematical designation ('X') for something unknown.

At one point while he was investigating the ability of various materials to stop the rays, Röntgen brought a small piece of lead into position while a discharge was occurring.

Röntgen thus saw the first radiographic image, his own flickering ghostly skeleton on the barium platinocyanide screen. He later reported that it was at this point that he determined to continue his experiments in secrecy, because he feared for his professional reputation if his observations were in error.

Nearly two weeks after his discovery, he took the very first picture using X-rays of his wife Anna Bertha's hand. When she saw her skeleton she exclaimed "I have seen my death!" Today, Röntgen is considered the father of diagnostic radiology, the medical speciality which uses imaging to diagnose disease.

Many people described his discovery as an accidental discovery that revolutionized medicine. This was not what he was looking for but was alert enough to the gentle nudge of destiny towards fluorescence which changed the world of medicine forever.

Freedom

You become free when you learn to hear your inner voice and don't get bothered by people's opinions.

You become free when it is not the destination which matters to you but the journey.

You become free when purpose in your life is bigger than winning or losing.

You become free when you are able to close your eyes and feel silence. Noise outside does not matter to you.

You become free, when you realise you have your own personal legend to achieve and you have the power to fulfil that legend.

You become free, when become receptive to universe's nudges which guide towards your destined path.

□

LEAP OF FAITH

In the preceding chapter you must be getting a feeling of fate or destiny playing a big role in where you reach in life. But that is not true. Nudges that I described in last section, play a big role in our journey but not everyone responds to the nudges in the same way. That response to the opportunities presented to us is in our control. That is what has been described in the holy books as '*Karma*'.

Let's rediscover the journeys that we discussed with a new perspective. What if Fleming saw the antibacterial action of penicillin but didn't go ahead

with examining it further. That decision to follow, or, not to follow a nudge rests with us. Choices that we make define our journey. What makes him great is the fact that he went ahead to examine, to understand. He didn't know that he was doing something great but still continued forward to explore. That is what I call as leap of faith. Usually, to take a leap of faith means "to believe in something with no evidence for it" or "to attempt an endeavour that has little chance of success." The leap of faith involves having a basic belief in yourself and a fundamental trust in the vision of who, what, and where you want to be in the future.

You might be wondering why would someone ignore a winning tip. But you will be surprised how often it happens in real life.

Let me unfold the reasons for this.

First and foremost is the 'Routine' or, 'Normalcy'.

Most innovative ideas and solutions are often staring at us but are often hidden by the routine. Something that you see everything your brain starts reading it as normal, or, routine. You don't want to redefine what is routine, or, not everyday. So, your brain develops a blind spot for the routine stuff and is only alerted if you see something different, or, an odd man out. Imagine a day when there is something unusual happening but you miss it because you were not looking at it. Your mind was pre-occupied with your routine and you missed the small aberration.

Now when you look back, do you think others didn't notice radiation illuminating the anode of Crooks tube? Do you think penicillium did not exist before Fleming? Do you think others didn't have an idea of a smart phone before Steve Jobs did? You know the answer.

You may not believe but when Steve Jobs unveiled iPhone, these were the reactions of the other thought leaders.

Mike Lazaridis, former CEO of RIM (now BlackBerry):

"Talk; all I'm [hearing] is talk about [the iPhone's chances in Enterprise]. I think it's important that we put this thing in perspective. Apple's design-centric approach [will] ultimately limit its appeal by sacrificing needed enterprise functionality. I think over-focus on one blinds you to the value of the other. ... Apple's approach produced devices that inevitably sacrificed advanced features for aesthetics."

Steve Ballmer, former CEO of Microsoft:

"You can get a Motorola Q for $99. [Apple] will have the most expensive phone, by far, in the marketplace. There's no chance that the iPhone is going to get any significant market share. No chance."

We have been trained to look for innovation looking like something exotic and often it comes to you in form of a slight aberration to the routine. Vast majority ends up passing it as routine.

Artists and scientists have one thing in common. They look at ordinary with a different eye than others. How many of ushave Marvelled at ordinary chair that Von Gogh painted? It is an ordinary chair, but he saw something in that and created a masterpiece.

(In 1888 Vincent van Gogh painted Van Gogh's Chair as an unusual portrait depicting himself. For his own portrait, van Gogh used one of the twelve simple chairs he had purchased when he furnished the Yellow House. His pipe and a pouch of tobacco on the rush seat and the box of onions that bears his name serve as rustic attributes that contrast to the more elegant items he chose to represent Paul Gauguin. The predominant hue in Van Gogh's Chair is yellow, which van Gogh now regarded as his signature colour).

In field of literature they often use a term 'De-Familiarisation'. What if you could deconstruct in your mind the routine, the ordinary. What if you could forget, what routine is. Then you would describe, or, depict everything as if you are seeing it for first time. You saw the trees swaying to wind and you felt the cool breeze touch you gently. You thought it to be routine yet the poet saw magic.

I often try this as an exercise. I look at my problem, or, my business with a third party perspective. Look at them as if, I am seeing them for first time. An uninvolved person would deconstruct things to understand what is going on and often an innovative solution would reveal to him that we were missing for routine.

Would it sound outrageous to you if I said most innovations were visible to many but most considered them to be a part of their ordinary routine and missed them.

An exercise which I believe, helps us all to tackle and re-assess the situation

we are in, is using the Third party perspective

We all have a distorted view of the problems.

I often meet youngsters who will come to me distressed over issues which are otherwise small, but they are being affected by it out of proportion. To help them see the things in correct perspective I often tell them about problems and roadblocks faced by great and famous people which were real challenges and I ask them about it. They are often surprised by their own response. They don't feel the same overwhelming response to a massive problem in someone else while their own trivial problems are appearing magnified.

May be we look at our problems from close and they magnify disproportionately. Then I ask them to look at their own issues dispassionately from a third party perspective and I ask them if they still feel they are distressed.

Often the issue is solved as soon as you learn to see things from a third party perspective. And apply correction to distorted magnified view of our current situation.

"Nobody understands how the world will change. The only way you can plan for the future is to have scenarios. You have to have the courage to take a leap of faith on one of them."

—Anand Mahindra

□

PASSION

The 'Mad' Energy

Madness of a certain kind gives you a disproportionate energy. This is massive, thrust of energy that you have, normal inhibited people calculating each move can never have this kind of energy. That is why you always associate the word passion, or, energy with creators, and high achievers. These are the people who are in pursuit of something extraordinary. Others will keep debating about the need to do it, should we do it, how many have done it before, what is risk involved, etc. People pursuing passion are ruled by a force, which gives them the 'mad' energy. Where they want to do things despite enduring pain, criticism and often self-neglect. But the forward momentum they can create is unparalleled.

I often define passion as creators 'mad' energy. Yes, you have to be mad enough to seek the harder life. Achievements sound good on paper but there is always a price to be paid and you need that mad energy to propel you.

You become a rocket, burning fuel to propel upward. Only thing that matter is achieving the escape velocity and reaching the space. Gravitational forces are similar to what you encounter in real life they massively pull you back. That is where passion is such an important component for success.

There is one thing common in all high achievers, they are greatly passionate about something be it music, theatre, art, medicine, teaching, technology, cause etc. Something triggers their imagination.

That something sparks their fuel somehow. But once sparked the engine roars like that of a Ferrari and they accelerate and they take off at a speed which others can only describe as mad.

But that momentum is the key to creation.

"In spurs of madness master pieces are created"

Another reason I call such passion as 'mad' energy because in such a spell the goal is not the driving force. The joy of doing the task is key force. And gets you to sculpt the creation again and again till you see perfection, then to find another fault and then again get back to work. You will hear all successful people talk about the journey not the destination. Many great achievers were never valued in their lifetime. They were so engrossed in their journey that they never seemed to bother.

Pain and prices on the way don't hurt because your passion matters.

End results don't matter because you have to be 'mad' enough to love what you do so much that rewards don't matter.

'Journey itself is the reward'

Do you feel the blood in your veins racing?

So many people seem to do things for the sake of doing them. With no enthusiasm, no energy and obviously no joy. They seem to be bound by compulsion, or, peer pressure. Truth is we all have limited time. We need to truly assess our acts and find out what we really need to do. Few years back I made a rule that I will not do things just for the sake of doing. I have to do things which set my blood racing. I have to give priority to my passion, my driving force, doing things that really trigger my adrenaline surge. Now, if I find myself in an event where I feel out of place and wasted, I decide to not repeat that mistake. I want to give my time to my priorities. That aligns my schedule, my time management.

Secret to success according to me is to consciously look for something triggers your imagination, something that does not feel like work burden, something that sets your blood racing and then of you find it, press the pedal. Not everyone gets a chance to coincide passion and work and if you get to that zone, push harder.

Many times I meet people who question me, "why should you take so much effort to do your work when after doing all this, still all you eat is normal food? "Do I actually have a reason for my efforts, and when I introspect and think, I realize it is the fire in my belly, the desire to win which pushes me to put that extra effort into all I do and go the extra mile. Most people who fail in achieving their goals in life are the people who don't have the desire to win, which may be because of two reasons –either choosing the wrong goal, or, lack of the proverbial 'fire in the belly'. These are the people who question why do athletes run, jump and push themselves to the limits, why did Sachin Tendulkar play the game for so long, even after records and money stopped mattering.

Reason is in the feeling you get at the moment of glory which the winners get addicted to. It is spurt of adrenaline surge, exhilaration, and moment of thrill which the athlete feels while crossing the line, and formula 1 racer feels when he sees the chequered flag. There is always a risk involved in stretching yourselves beyond your limits but desire to win outweighs all the risk and doubts. It is not true that winners don't have self-doubts, they win despite doubts. Everybody's life is like a see-saw where there are phases when we feel low and phases when we want to touch the stars. You have to find something that fires your imagination, and then go all out for your moment of glory. There are always many reasons not to play but there is only reason to play, the desire to win. You can remain static and safe forever theoretically speaking, but as Napoleon said, 'a moment of glory is worth more than a lifetime of obscurity.

Most people dream about big things but don't go ahead with them for various reasons. After having talked with lacs of students I feel there are two main barriers to proceeding further. First one is fear.

This is a feeling of being overwhelmed by the dream itself. You start feeling about the odds ratios and probability of winning. It is obvious when you seek something big, examples of success will be few and defeat will be more. This fear induces a paralysing effect which makes you question your ability and whether you deserve to win or not. This fear is the factor that most people give up.

Somehow you have to learn to black out this fear. Most important method here is to put the dream to the back of your mind. What is a dream, it is the destination that you envision for yourself but is not time bound. If somehow you breakdown your dream into smaller time bound targets and tasks, and put them in the front of your mind. Now you are not looking at an overwhelming dream all the time as it is now in the back of your mind. You are looking at a doable target for the week. Each target finished will give you a sense of completion. And all winners acknowledge the value of this sense of completion. After significant number of targets are achieved that is when you push the pedal because you see the possibility. You smell victory and your heart tells you move forward with a force. That is end of the first barrier.

During this phase of hard-work you start experiencing the second barrier, that is pain. Real life success needs hard work. You cannot win it in a lottery or inherit it. Examples in history abound where famous fathers didn't exactly translate into son's success. When you work you feel pain. Same thing happens when you go to a gymnasium. You like the muscular bodies that film stars flaunt but when you start working, you experience pain. Journey of the people with high ambition is not easy. It calls for sacrifices both personal and at relationship level. You don't make a dent in the universe if you don't give up on certain things. You cannot be wasting your time gossiping when you have a bigger dream in mind. At times, when others would be talking of parties, cricket matches, Netflix, you would be wondering why are you working so hard. To give you an example, I have never watched big boss series, or, game of thrones and often I see youngsters making a fuss over it, there is nothing right or wrong here, but when you aim high you need to give your time

GOT

to dreams. This pain of hard-work, pain of giving up on apparently pleasurable activities, and at times demanding relationships lead to many people giving up.

Battle of life reveals the true you: Most important person to understand in life is your own self. We appear to have an idea about ourselves but that perception is often coloured by aspirations and experiences. You apparently perceive yourself to be larger than life, someone who can do it all but then the battle of life begins. You face challenges that hit you with fear and pain. They expose you. You react in a way you never thought you would. You see areas in your mind that you never knew existed. You see peaks and troughs like never before. Even though you are suffering, you are in a unique zone of self-realisation, that is unparalleled. You know what you are. Some of us, at that moment are able to rise from the ashes. To do the impossible.

We emerge from the battle scarred but enlightened. Seeking another battle. You get to know your true warrior self. You were afraid, you felt pain but that is what you are 'the warrior' and your true self exists in the battlefield.

You are destined for the battle. You need to live your destiny. And you will come back a changed person

These two barriers of fear and pain lead most people to give up on their dreams. But that is not it. When you give up at this point you create regrets. Yes, the most poisonous substance you can accumulate in your soul is regret. You may not acknowledge it. You may act unconcerned to people. You may tell others how irrelevant dreams are but there is one person you cannot fool, and that is 'you'. Your heart knows it. You know it that you messed up. You choked when it mattered most.

This is where understanding the concept of passion will help you.

Sometimes a youngster would walk to me saying he is interested in cricket. I ask him what do you about it. He says, I watch cricket on TV and I have never missed any match. I said great, what else do you do. He said I am studying to be a Doctor. I smiled and told him that it seems to me that cricket is your interest not passion. Many people mistake interest for passion. Passion is a pursuit that makes you forget everything else. The pain, the fear and other activities. One activity that gives you true joy. Once I was listening to an interview by Sachin Tendulkar, greatest batsman of all times, he was asked what do you enjoy most, mind you he has everything money, Ferrari which most people feel are important, but his answer was he loves the sound of ball hitting middle of the bat is the one which gives him maximum joy. He has practising and playing cricket since childhood and it would mean waking up early and practise. Many people would

2011
INDIA

want to be him but not his path. That is what differentiates passion from interest. Passion makes you oblivious of price you pay. It acts as a propelling force. Now if we connect the dots we started with a nudge, a subconscious push towards your destined path, if you have courage to believe that blurred picture you take the leap of faith, but continuing forward needs energy. An extraordinary force which can propel you. Only thing that matters is the dream. There will be forces and factors holding you back but that joy in the activity overrules everything else.

Sachin Ramesh Tendulkar (born 24 April 1973) is a former Indian international cricketer and a former captain of the Indian national team. He is widely regarded as one of the greatest batsman in the history of cricket. He is the highest run scorer of all time in International cricket. Tendulkar took up cricket at the age of eleven, made his Test debut on 15 November 1989 against

Pakistan in Karachi at the age of sixteen, and went on to represent Mumbai domestically and India internationally for close to twenty-four years. He is the only player to have scored one hundred international centuries, the first batsman to score a double century in an ODI, the holder of the record for the most number of runs in both Test and ODI, and the only player to complete more than 30,000 runs in international cricket. He is colloquially known as Little Master, or, Master Blaster.

How many of you remember that India-England match in India where the English team won and did a victory lap after removing their shirts because of they were sweating in Indian heat. One man did not like it. One man was hurt. He was our beloved passionate captain of that time Sourav Ganguly. Later when India toured England, Indian team paid back by winning in the lords cricket ground, the Mecca of cricket. Sourav in a historic and often infamous move after winning, took off his shirt in cold English winner and waved it. That is passion for you. The desire to achieve dreams irrespective of the price you pay in the end. That one act sums up the man Sourav is. And probably the reason why he is the man credited with changing the Indian outfit to an aggressive unit. Man full of passionate energy, tirelessly working towards a dream is a story that everyone loves but hard to emulate for everyone because passion makes you blind to other things, which might even be health, or, relationships. But this man who is now a rocket has a mission to achieve escape velocity to fly into the space. Sceptics will see him burning but he is only bothered about the mission.

SouravGanguly (born 8 July 1972), affectionately known as Dada (meaning 'elder brother' in Bengali), is former cricketer and captain of the Indian national team, Currently, he is

appointed as the President of the Cricket Association of Bengal. During his playing career, Ganguly established himself as one of the world's leading batsmen and also one of the greatest captains of the national cricket team. While batting, he was especially prolific through the off side, earning himself the nickname God of the Off Side for his elegant stroke-play square of the wicket and through the covers.

Indian fans erupted in joy. The cameras panned to the Lord's dressing room where the players celebrated in delight. Sourav Ganguly emerged from behind VVS Laxman, took his shirt off and celebrated the win. He was roaring in delight. It was him who laid the foundation... not just for the chase in the big final but for an Indian team that would go on to become world beaters in the following years.

Here's the conversation Ganguly had with Boycott in the commentary box.

Boycott: "You must mention your experience about taking your jersey off and flying it in the air at the Mecca of Cricket: Lord's! Ohhh, you naughty boy!"

Ganguly: "One of your boys (Andrew Flintoff) also took off his jersey here in Mumbai."

Boycott: "Yeah, but Lord's is the Mecca of cricket."

Ganguly: "Lord's is your Mecca, and Wankhede is ours!"

Famous line written by Kurt Cobain, lead singer of rock band, Nirvana, the band which ruled the world of Rock music in 1990s, "I would rather burn, then fade away", kind of explains the passionate pursuit.

Kurt Cobain (February 20, 1967 – April 5, 1994) was an American singer, songwriter, and musician, best known as the guitarist and frontman of the rock band Nirvana. He is remembered as one of the most iconic and influential rock musicians in the history of alternative music. Born in Aberdeen, Washington, Cobain formed the band Nirvana with Krist Novoselic and Aaron Burckhard in 1987 and established it as part of the Seattle music scene which later became known as grunge. After signing with major label DGC Records, Nirvana found success with 'Smells Like Teen Spirit' from their second album Never mind (1991). Following the success of Never mind, Nirvana was labelled 'the flagship band' of Generation X, and Cobain was hailed as 'the spokesman of a generation'.

The universe loves the passionate pursuit. These are people who believe in the impossible. They are different from sceptical intelligentsia. They are full of positive energy and massively optimistic. They might get hurt, they might lose a few battles but they continue onwards irrespective. Optimism is a quality which you associate with winners. Are they optimistic because they are winners, or, they are winners because of optimism?

It is probably the later. Because you will put in more, when you believe. And universe loves them, they are creators, entrepreneurs, doers, people who do magic and bring about a change. Universe tends to help them. Yes, we all have heard of the famous quote about entire universe helping you in your journey, but that happens when you are enjoying the journey itself.

Let me add an adjective to passion, detachment. I called it 'Detached Passion'.

This is one of the most underrated aspect which determines your success. We all agree on the role passion and hard work play in your achieving anything in life. But then, why some passionate and hardworking people are not able to make it? I feel Answer to this lies in being passionate about something but you need to have the ability to detach yourselves from the results. It will sound paradoxical.

How can you practise detachment

when you are so passionate about something.

Probably answer can be understood by observing sportsmen, the modern day gladiators try their best to win the game they are passionate about. They put their all in the game but if you notice them closely as soon as they lose some games they just walk up to the net, congratulate the opponent, and walk off to yet another battle somewhere else. They train to switch off their mind to previous loss. Else they cannot give their 110% in the next game.

This is what I call as 'detached passion'.

That's the real secret of success, to play as if the world depends on the game, give all you have mentally and emotionally to the cause and then go on to the next cause without getting overwhelmed by success or failure.

'Passionate for the cause'

'But detached from the results'

Have you ever been to an administrative office for some paperwork, probably a 10 minutes job. You meet some people who seem to be just looking at the clock, just to see the time passing. Just waiting for the clock to strike 4 pm and get freedom.

Have you ever seen the excitement for the Friday night around you? They all seem so happy that the work is ending. Then seeking desperate ways to pass time on the weekend. The need to do something, live, before the work starts again. Then on Monday the wait for Friday begins all over again.

Have you ever wondered, we spend a significant proportion of our time at work. What if you could find something in life which is your work but does not seem like work? What if you were pursuing something that enjoy doing and each day was an enjoyable journey itself? What if you don't feel the need to look at the clock at all? What if you loved the journey itself and destination hardly mattered?

Hoping you find a journey that does not seem like work and if you do find, don't look back.

PURPOSE

Unlike animals, which are driven by instinctive survival, we crave more from life than mere survival. Without an answer to the question 'Survival for what? We can fall into disillusionment, distraction and a sense of despair. The most powerful driver of our life is purpose. There will be times when everything seems to be going wrong. You will feel helpless and out of control. Despite all advancements in the world often we find ourselves to be part of scenarios which are beyond our control. We try hard to control and dictate the terms, yet harder we try, more we suffer. Imagine someone in chronic illness where the best doctors can offer is symptomatic relief but not cure. Imagine someone chasing a justice system offering them date after date. You seek help outside but their words sound hollow and reassurances plastic. German philosopher Frederick Nietzsche said, 'He who has a why can endure anyhow.'

That is the time to look inside. Introspect, find what really matters to you.

You cannot control the situation but you can always manage your reaction.

Find your purpose.

Chasing that one thing gives you deep satisfaction and sense of worth fullness.

You matter despite all your problems.

You exist for a reason and that reason is purpose.

Our guiding light is our life purpose. We cannot thrive until we discover it; and we cannot fail to thrive as long as we align ourselves with it every day.

Purpose is not a big, or, audacious goal. It is a bridge between your unique gifts and what the world wants most from you. Purpose of your life is who you are when you feel most alive, most useful, most awake. I feel most alive while teaching and I know now my purpose in life is not about money, or, fame that I make. It is the unique sense of being awake I feel during my lecture to medical students. I feel useful, I feel alive.

This purpose is unique to you. It cannot be right, or, wrong. It cannot be judged upon by other, or, vice versa. Purpose is the creative you, free from limitations and helps you and others thrive. I find it difficult to articulate in words what my purpose is, but I do feel it. I feel that I have a purpose. And that is the most important thing. You need to feel it.

In a world full of noise and chaos we all need a sacred secret space where we feel most resonant with our innerself.

No, I don't mean that we lock ourselves up in a cave, or, go to the mountains. That space is inside us, and it reveals to us when we are engrossed in the activity that means most to us. I have often noticed a sense of calm comes over to me after long teaching activity gets over, and that calm is accompanied by a sense of silent joy, not the euphoria kind, subtle joy and feeling of worth fullness. I assume similar feelings are experience by surgeons, cardiologists, painters, artists, engineers, architects when they are totally immersed in what they are doing and completion gives them the silent joy. You know the most about yourself in that zone. You feel connected to the energy of the universe, you feel you are making a difference.

That space, that zone in your mind, is your sacred space, your purpose.

Hold on to it.

Learn to relish your moments in that zone.

In the end that is all that matters.

I feel difficulty in finding words to describe my feeling. To me whatever I am doing in DAMS is my expression of my purpose. My purpose, or, most useful I feel when I am teaching. I searched the internet and stumbled upon a Japanese term which probably best described what I am trying to describe, 'Ikigai'

Ikigai is a Japanese concept that means 'a reason for being'. The word 'ikigai' is usually used to indicate the source of value in one's life, or, the things that make one's life worthwhile. The word translated to English roughly means 'thing that you live for' or, 'the reason for which you wake up in the morning'. Each individual's ikigai is personal to them and specific to their lives, values and beliefs. It reflects the inner self of an individual and expresses that faithfully, while simultaneously creating a mental state in which the individual feels at ease. Activities that allow one to feel ikigai are never forced on an individual; they are often spontaneous, and always undertaken willingly, giving the individual satisfaction and a sense of meaning to life. Kobayashi Tsukasa says that "people can feel real ikigai only when, on the basis of personal maturity, the satisfaction of various desires, love and happiness, encounters with others, and a sense of the value of life, they proceed toward self-realization".

Another term which I came across is 'Logotherapy'. Logotherapy is a decades-old psychotherapeutic approach developed by Viktor Frankl. The driving force behind logotherapy is the idea that human beings are most motivated by a search for meaning, indicating that the meaning of life is the biggest question on our minds and the biggest stressor on our psyches. Rather than power, or, pleasure, logotherapy is founded upon the belief that striving to find meaning in life is the primary, most powerful motivating and driving force in humans. A short introduction to this system is given in Frankl's most famous book, Man's Search for Meaning, in which he outlines how his theories helped him to survive his Holocaust experience and how that experience further developed and reinforced his theories. The notion of Logotherapy was created with the Greek word logos ('reason'). Frankl's concept is based on the premise that the primary motivational force of an individual is to find a meaning in life.

Viktor Frankl was born March 26, 1905 and died September 2, 1997, in Vienna, Austria. He was influenced during his early life by Sigmund Freud and Alfred Adler, earned a medical degree from the University of Vienna Medical School in 1930. From 1940 to 1942, he was the director of the Neurological Department of the Rothschild Hospital, and from 1946 to 1970 was the director of the Vienna Polyclinic of Neurology.

In 1942, Frankl was deported to a Nazi concentration camp along with his wife, parents, and other family members. He spent time in four camps in total, including Auschwitz, from 1942 to 1945, and was the only member of his family to survive. In 1945, he returned to Vienna and published a book on his theories, based on his records of observations during his time in the camps. By the time of his death, his book, "Man's Search for Meaning" had been published in 24 languages.

In a nutshell, what he says is:

"Life has meaning under all circumstances, even the most miserable ones."

"Our main motivation for living is our will to find meaning in life."

"We have freedom to find meaning in what we do, and what we experience, or, at least in the stance we take when faced with a situation of unchangeable suffering"

We all have seen a photograph of man digging a tunnel and just before he could have got the treasure, he gives up. Let me examine what happened in his life before and after the event.

Before

He heard stories about the adventure and thrill of chasing a treasure. As a child he would get up in night dreaming about all those treasure stories. He would go find a treasure once he grows up, he promised. This was his mission in life.

He did get his chance. One day he heard about the hidden treasure buried in the street near his city. He took this as a divine signal and decided to go for it. It was a vast area and he had scarce means. He was undeterred. Day in and day out he would dig at different sites. Trying to understand each of the divine signals. Months and years passed. Failure after failure he got irritable. Family and friends initially took pity on him and then left him. He had lost it. There are no treasures they tried to convince him. But he was in a mad pursuit.

On that day

This particular day was particularly hot day. He felt extremely low today. Lack of proper food had made him weak and failures had made him angry. Grumbling and mumbling he was digging in tunnel. He was digging but was losing hope. What if all of it was lie. He thought of all the lost days of life. May be people were

right. He heard the loud noise from birds nearby. Was jealous of their freedom. He was but a prisoner of his dreams. Suddenly, he left the shovel and decided to give up. No more pursuit now. I want to live like others, watching soap opera, drinking and enjoying. His head became heavy and came back to his city with a heavy heart. Little did he know he was just an inch away from his dreams, his treasure. There was no way he could know. Universe screamed to tell him but he was already determined to give up.

Afterwards

He was now a different man. He would frown at any mention of treasures or dreams. He has the guilt of giving up but he also believed that there are no treasures. He would laugh when someone told him about other explorers finding treasures. He would tell others to prefer life over dreams. He had a secret regret inside and was a changed man.

People who knew him before, described as a man who had dried up. No emotions no ambitions, just mechanical. May be he was now adapted to the real world. May be this was the truth. May be there are no treasures.

Seems like we all are digging our own tunnels and giving up is worst we can ever do, we never know how near we were to the joy of discovery and treasures we seek.

There will be moments in life where you see the futility of it all. You don't want to talk to people about it because you already know that they wouldn't understand. You don't see sense in your behaviour but you tend to seek negativity. There is cold, gloomy darkness everywhere. You want to carry on but days and nights are passing by quickly with your realising. You want the days to brighten up and long for someone else to take initiative, you are just not upto it to seek it yourself. That is where is

340
0
20
40
N.E
60
E
N

you need to stop yourself from sinking. You change focus to small, achievable goals to achieve, one's which are doable and finishing them consciously seek joy. Focus on feeling good for small achievements. Talking in itself may seem useless but it offers you catharsis. A way to unburden yourself and when you speak to others you speak to yourself as well. Audit your activity and find something doing which gives you a sense of achievement, completion and gives you maximum satisfaction. Consciously doing that activity will bring back your self-esteem and remind you that you are valuable. Don't be too heavy on yourself and your past. You did what you could. Remind yourself about your 'Why', your purpose and have faith on your personal legend. You deserve to happy. You are there for a purpose.

If I have to put all that I have learnt so far in four lines, it would be-

- It all begins with subconscious Nudges.
- Then, needs the courage to take the leap of the faith.
- Passion is the driving fuel.
- When everything else fails, the purpose remains.

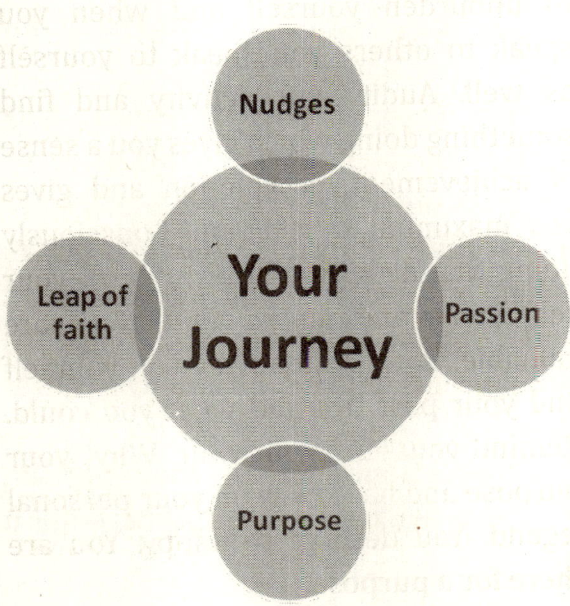

What is the solution to my problem?

It is inside us.

- We all seek solutions to problems we are facing in the outside world.
- We all feel this or that person is responsible for my problems.
- We all blame the system, the organisation and what not for our issues.

But then, if you introspect, look within, you discover it is within us.

Both the problem and the solution.

At those moments often you get an insight on how you should take it forward and if you follow that instinct, bingo the problem disappears, as if it was never there.

It was a mountain in the mind and now you don't even see it. Where did it go?

It was not outside.

It was inside.